Farming
Then and Now

Written by Charles R. Smith Jr.

Illustrated by Jessika von Innerebner

Acknowledgments
The publisher would like to thank the following for their kind permission to reproduce their photographs:(Key: b-bottom; c-center; l-left; r-right; t-top) **123RF.com:** Cary Bates 8tr, clinton weaver 8br, nito500 10cr, Witold Krasowski 10c; **Alamy Images:** DP RM 3bl, 14-15c, geogphotos 3br, 6, 13tr, nsf 13bc, Scott Sinklier 2br, 9, Terry Mathews 7, The Keasbury-Gordon Photograph Archive 2bc, 12bc, 15tr, travelib environment 2bl, 8tl, Universal Images Group Limited 16, Wolstenholme Images 4-5c; **Getty Images:** Haeckel collection / ullstein bild 3bc, 11bc, Maeers / Fox Photos 10bc; **Shutterstock.com:** Dja65 6c, 8c, 10cl, 12, Mariusz Szczygiel 11tr, Richard Williamson 4l

Cover images: *Front:* **Alamy Images:** Alan Fern 02, The Keasbury-Gordon Photograph Archive 03, Wolstenholme Images 1.

All other images © Pearson Education.

PEARSON

ISBN-13: 978-0-328-83268-2
ISBN-10: 0-328-83268-5

15   19

Printed in Mexico

Contents

Time to Wake Up

A day on the farm starts when the sun rises. There are lots of chores to be done on the farm. The first chore of the day is to milk the cows.

Did You Know?

Most of the time, farmers get up at daybreak and work until the sun goes down. That can be twelve hours a day!

Things on the farm weren't always like they are now. I'll show you. Let's take Great Grampy's secret pocket watch and travel back through time.

Let's go!

POOF!

Time to Milk the Cows

One hundred years ago, most milking was done by hand one cow at a time.

THEN

Did You Know?

A cow makes about 44 pints of milk per day.

Time to Feed the Animals

One hundred years ago, animals ate cut-up turnips, potatoes, beets, and other root vegetables in the winter after the hay was gone.

Did You Know?

Alfalfa is one of the most nutritious crops that animals eat. It is also the oldest known plant used as animal feed.

NOW

Today, animals such as cows and sheep eat silage in the winter. This is a type of food made from grass crops such as corn.

To make silage, you need to harvest the crops. Let's see how this has changed over time.

Time to Harvest

One hundred years ago, it took **24** workers using scythes and sickles a whole day to cut five acres of barley or wheat. That's bigger than three football fields put together!

THEN

scythe

sickle

That's a lot of work!

Today, a combine harvester can cut twenty acres of wheat in one hour.

Did You Know?

In the past, people often celebrated the end of the harvest with music, parades, and a large feast.

Time to Shear the Sheep

In the spring we shear the sheep to keep them cool.

One hundred years ago, it took two people to shear a sheep. One would spin the wheel to drive the clippers, and the other would shear the sheep.

Today, one person can shear a sheep using electric clippers like those used for a haircut.

Did You Know?

The world record for one person shearing sheep is 866 sheep in 9 hours — that's around 96 sheep per hour!

Wow! That's about one and a half sheep per minute!

Then or Now?

Life on a farm was hard before there were machines. I'm glad I live on a farm now.

Not me! I think it would have been fun! There were more people working on the farm back then to talk to.

Some things on the farm never change. Such as getting up at daybreak and working until the sun goes down.

Glossary

alfalfa	type of plant that animals eat
crops	plants grown on a farm
nutritious	healthy to eat
scythe	sharp, curved tool with a long handle for cutting crops
shear	to cut the hair or fur of an animal
sickle	sharp, curved tool with a short handle for cutting crops
silage	grass that is cut and stored over the winter